HOW TO WRITE A COMPOSITION

HOW TO WRITE A COMPOSITION

BERTHA DAVIS

ILLUSTRATIONS BY ANNE CANEVARI GREEN

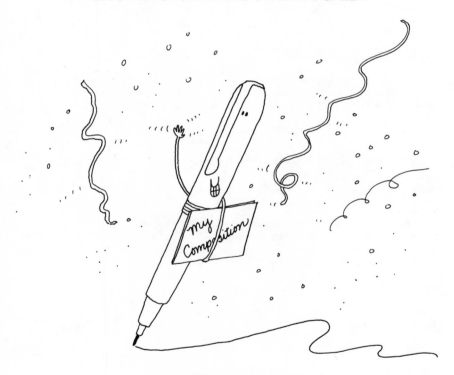

FRANKLIN WATTS
New York/London/Toronto/Sydney
1985
A First Book

Index cards displayed on pp. 39–40 are used with permission of
Macmillan Publishing Company from Learning Lab for *The Ways of Man:
An Introduction To Many Cultures* by John Jarolimek and Bertha Davis.
Copyright © 1974 Macmillan Publishing Company.

Examples of student compositions on pp. 71–75 are taken from New York
State Education Department, Bureau of English and Reading, *Packet for
the Training of Raters for the New York State Preliminary Competency
Test in Writing.*

Library of Congress Cataloging in Publication Data

Davis, Bertha, 1910–
How to write a composition.

(A First book)
Summary: A step-by-step plan for developing writing
skills for use not only as a student but later in
business, professional, and community life.
1. English language—Composition and exercises—
Juvenile literature.   [1. English language—Composition
and exercises]   I. Green, Anne Canevari, ill.
II. Title.
PE1408.D238   1985   808'.042   85-8817
ISBN 0-531-10042-1

CONTENTS*

* For the reader who is concerned with specific kinds of writing, the table of
contents lists these. For example, if you need information about persuasive
writing, you will find the subject listed under chapters 1, 2, 5, and 6.

HOW TO WRITE A COMPOSITION

INTRODUCTION

The title of this book is somewhat misleading. It could have been

How to Go About Writing Almost Anything You Will Need or Want to Write in School, in College, in Business and Professional Life, and in Carrying on Personal Business

But titles are supposed to be brief.

Practically everything that is written is meant to be read by someone other than the writer. True, some people do keep diaries that they want no eyes but their own to see. A very few express their thoughts and feelings in writing that no one sees, simply because the act of writing gives them pleasure or helps them sort out their thoughts. But granted these and other possible exceptions, practically everything is written to get action from someone, or to convey one's thoughts and feelings to others, or to inform, to entertain, to persuade someone other than the writer. If the writing is good, it accomplishes its purpose. Poor writing, on the other hand, is ineffective.

The student who does assigned writing tasks effectively is rewarded by the response of others who see his or her work—and by good grades. But how important is the ability to communicate effectively in writing when the days of being graded are over?

Ask someone who has had some success in business, or an attorney, or an engineer, or a public official, or an adult who is active in community affairs. Ask these questions:

- Do you ever have to write anything to inform someone about something? to explain something? to persuade someone to do something or believe something?
- Does writing ability help to bring success in your line of work? in your everyday life?

You will find that now and in the future it will be extremely useful to approach any writing task with the confidence that comes with writing skill. Building that writing skill is the purpose of this book.

1

IDENTIFYING THE WRITING TASK

Effective writing begins with identifying the writing task. Identifying the writing task begins with the question; What kind of writing am I being asked to do?

IDENTIFYING THE KIND OF WRITING REQUIRED

Here are some writing tasks that you are likely to be called on to do in the upper elementary and junior high school grades.

● Write a one- or two-paragraph composition on one of the following topics, or a similar topic of your own choice:

Watching a scary movie
Cleaning my room
Returning to school after summer vacation

- Write a composition on the topic: "How I Feel About..." Complete the title with a subject from this list: science labs, collecting things, sidewalk vendors, break dancing—or a subject of your own choice.

- Write a composition using one of the following titles:

  An Empty House
  Country Roads
  City Streets
  Thoughts on a Holiday

- Write a one- or two-paragraph description of one of the following, or choose your own person, place, or thing to describe:

  An outdoor scene
  A family pet
  A scene of destruction
  Something you would like to own
  A person you like/dislike

The four assignments above are worded differently, but all require the same kind of writing. All require the writer to express feelings, emotions, reactions, thoughts, the way he or she sees persons or places. We will refer to that kind of writing as "personal compositions" because the writer is required to supply personal raw material.

The next two assignments also require personal compositions but they differ from those above in an important way. Tasks like these require you, as the writer, to draw on your knowledge, what you know. Here your purpose is to inform your readers, rather than to share feelings, thoughts, emotions with the readers for their pleasure or amusement.

- Choose from the list below a subject with which you are familiar. Write a composition of 150–200 words to introduce that subject to readers of your age who know nothing about it.

    Computer games
    The scientific method
    The guidance program in your school

- Write a 150–200-word composition explaining to readers of your own age how to make something or do something that you know how to make or do.

A separate chapter in this book will be devoted to the kind of writing to inform that is based on reading or other kinds of investigation, that is, a research paper. Writing whose purpose is to inform becomes more and more important as you move on through school and into the adult world. For example, students in high school and college are often asked to write answers on examinations that are really compositions that set forth what they know about something.

Now here are two other examples of writing tasks that you often meet:

- Write a two- or three-paragraph account of

    A Happening that I wish hadn't happened
    The day I won the contest
    The day our team brought home the trophy
    An afternoon at a ballet rehearsal

    or tell the story of a personal experience of your own choice.

- Write a composition of about 150 words that answers one of the questions below, or a similar question of your own choice:

   In what ways is your school like/unlike schools shown on TV?
   How are the students in your class like/unlike the students in the grade above (or below) yours?

The first of the tasks listed above calls for narrative writing, that is a story of events, experiences, or the like that can be true or created by the imagination. The second calls for a comparison and spells out that comparing means telling ways in which things, places, people, or ideas are alike and ways in which they are unlike.

The next two examples of writing tasks require a challenging kind of writing—writing that tries to persuade the reader to do something or to accept a point of view.

- Write a letter to the editor of your local newspaper urging that interscholastic football be dropped from or added to the sports program of the local high school. Or choose a subject related to your own school on which there is controversy in the community and write a letter that states and defends your position on that subject.
- Your school newspaper has a column called "Our Readers Write Us." Write a letter to the column editor on one of these subjects or a similar subject of your own choice:

   The need for new clothing lockers
   Why our school should or should not buy more computers

You will easily recognize the last two examples as writing tasks that require, in turn, a business letter and a book report:

- Your social studies class is working on a unit on Latin America. Your teacher calls attention to an article in the local newspaper reporting on the recent return of Ms. Hermine Jaspar, a retired local business executive, from a trip to Argentina and Chile. Your teacher suggests that each member of the class write a letter to Ms. Jaspar inviting her to visit your class to talk about her trip. The assignment concludes with the promise that "the best letter will be sent to Ms. Jaspar."
- Choose one of the novels on the list posted in the Library Corner and write a 150–200-word book report on it. Later the reports will be kept in the Library Corner as a source of suggestions for books your classmates might want to read just for fun.

The writing tasks illustrated above do not exhaust the kinds of writing people do. Poetry was not mentioned, nor personal letters, nor diaries and journals, nor news articles, nor plays. But if you can handle the kinds of writing that were introduced, the kinds that will be taught in this book, you will be well on your way to achieving writing competence.

In the longer writing tasks that you will be called on to do in later years—a college term paper, a business proposal, for example—there may be some narrative, some description, lots of informing, some persuading, all in one paper. No matter. Once you have learned how to handle each kind you can handle a combination of kinds.

Identifying the kind of writing called for in twelve different assignments has taken a bit of time. But normally you have only one writing assignment before you. You identify the kind of writing required in that assignment; then, to complete your understanding of the writing task, you consider the answer to a second question: Who will be the audience for this piece of writing?

IDENTIFYING THE AUDIENCE

In the two personal compositions intended to inform, the audience was named as "readers of your age." The letter to the editor of the local newspaper would have as its audience the adult readers of that paper, while the audience for the letter to the "Our Readers Write Us" column would be the students in your school. The audience for the business letter is, of course, Ms. Jaspar, the retired business executive to whom the letter is written. The book report, the assignment makes clear, is intended for your classmates' use.

When no audience is defined in a school writing assignment you should assume that the audience is the other students in your class and your teacher.

A writer must identify his or her audience before starting a writing plan because the plan must fit the audience. Arguments to convince adults might well be different from those that would appeal to fellow students. Furthermore, when a writer gets to the actual writing of the paper, he or she adjusts the style to the audience, as we shall see. There is a time to be chatty and informal and a time to be businesslike and serious.

Now, with the required kind of writing pinned down and the audience identified, pre-writing planning can begin.

2

PRE-WRITING PLANNING USING BUILT-IN FRAMEWORKS

Since you know that "pre" means before, you know that this chapter will be about the planning that must go on before a piece of writing is undertaken. All writing needs planning. Writers at every level of skill, before they write anything longer than, say, a one-sentence note, think about the points they want to make and about the best order in which to make them. If they do not, the writing will not be as effective as it could have been.

Needless to say, all experienced writers do not plan in the same way. By the time you are an experienced writer, you may have worked out your own tricks of the trade. But until you reach that stage, the planning suggestions in this chapter and the next will serve you well.

Some kinds of writing assignments are easier to plan than others because there are ready-made planning frameworks available for those kinds of writing. Take narrative or experience writing, for example.

PRE-WRITING PLANNING OF NARRATIVE/EXPERIENCE COMPOSITIONS

From about grade four on, students are rarely asked to write the kind of narratives worked with in the early grades, such as "Draw a picture of a strange animal and write a story about an adventure he had one day." For that kind of assignment a third-grader can follow a simple formula: Tell what happened first; then tell what happened next; then what happened next; then what happened last.

Upper-grade narrative writing is likely to be accounts of personal experiences. In personal experience compositions the writer is expected to do more than tell what happened first, second, and third. The writer is expected to weave into the experience his or her feelings and reactions as the experience unfolded.

A useful way to start the planning of an experience composition is to think of the experience this way: Suppose someone had followed me through my experience with a TV camera. What scenes would be shown. For example, when Mary had to write an experience composition, she decided to tell about going to a ballet rehearsal. She decided that if someone were making a TV movie of her visit, the first "scene" would be in the lobby of the theater where the visitors were prepared for what they would see; then the camera would show the visitors in their seats watching what was going on on stage while the dancers waited for the rehearsal to begin; the final scene would be the rehearsal itself with the camera going back and forth between the dancers on stage and Mary's face as she watched. These three scenes became the major divisions of Mary's composition.

Having identified the major divisions or scenes of the experience, the writer then jots down notes, brief reminders of the details to be included in writing about each scene. The reason for the suggestion to think of scenes rather than a sequence of events is that that kind of thinking is more likely to make the writer recall colorful details that a movie camera would focus on.

So Mary's plan for her experience composition looked like this:

An Afternoon at a Ballet Rehearsal	
1. Lobby of theater—visitors being prepared to watch rehearsal	What ballets to be rehearsed Behavior during rehearsal Entering dark theater
2. In balcony of theater, waiting for rehearsal to start	Dancers' outfits Dancers' warm-ups Stagehands at work
3. Watching dancers at work	Appearance of director; low-key approach Different levels of activity— some dancing all out, some walking through Ironing out trouble spots Magic moments

In other words, this is the framework for a narrative/experience composition:

FRAMEWORK FOR A
NARRATIVE/EXPERIENCE COMPOSITION

Topic goes here	
Scenes	*Details*
Make as	many
boxes as	scenes

As you think through the experience, jotting down details to fill in your framework of scenes, you decide what your writing purpose will be. Almost all pieces of writing include, early in the piece, a sentence that states the writer's purpose, point, or theme. A sentence like this is often called the thesis statement.

Think of the statement of purpose or thesis statement for an experience composition as the answer to this question: Why am I telling this experience? Of course nine times out of ten you are telling the experience because you are required to do so. But that motive aside, it helps to write down the message you want to get across about the experience. Figuring out what that message is will help you write a better composition.

For example, from the details Mary listed in her writing plan she decided that the message she would try to get across—her thesis statement—would be this: A ballet rehearsal helps a ballet-goer understand how wonderful performances are created. Can you see that if she uses that sentence at the beginning of her composition it will show the reader that this writer really has something to say and that it might be interesting to find out what that something is?

Here is another example of how useful it is to write down your writing purpose. Eleanor and Fred wrote experience compositions based on their class trip to the planetarium. Eleanor made a writing plan like Mary's and thought about the message she wanted to communicate to her readers. Fred did no preplanning and simply wrote a first-we-did-this, then-this, then-this composition. Here are the opening sentences of the two compositions:

"Last week our class went to the planetarium."

"The sky will never look the same to me after
our trip to the planetarium."

Which sentence do you think is Fred's? Eleanor's? Which one sounds as if the writer has something interesting to say? Which one would you prefer to read?

PRE-WRITING PLANNING
OF PERSUASIVE COMPOSITIONS

There is also a built-in framework for writing that is intended to persuade. Here is an example of how Larry used it. One of the writing assignments listed in chapter 1 called for writing a letter to the editor of a school newspaper column arguing for new clothing lockers. Larry began his plan for the letter by writing a sentence that expressed the idea he was going to try to "sell" to the readers of the column. Here it is: "The Board of Education should provide funds for the school to buy additional clothing lockers." Then he jotted down three arguments or reasons to persuade his readers, and for each one he noted the details he would include to support the argument. His writing plan looked like this:

The Board of Education should provide funds for the school to buy additional clothing lockers.	
1. Numbers of students vs. number of hall lockers	600 students, 450 lockers Some broken locks Some rusty doors
2. Students wearing outdoor clothing inside	Health Appearance Arguments with teachers
3. Students allowed to use closets in classrooms	Interrupted classes Teachers with keys not around

In other words, the framework for any kind of persuasive writing is:

**FRAMEWORK FOR
PERSUASIVE WRITING**

Put here a sentence that expresses what the writing piece will try to persuade the audience to do or to believe.	
Reasons	*Details*
Reason 1.	
Reason 2.	
Reason 3	

Must Larry now prepare a thesis statement as Mary did after completing the writing plan for the experience composition? No. The opinion statement that tells what you will try to persuade the audience to do or to believe is the message, the statement of purpose, the thesis.

PRE-WRITING PLANNING OF COMPARISONS

There are two frameworks for writing tasks that call for comparisons of persons, places, things, events, ideas. Suppose Timothy is planning a comparison of his city school building and his friend George's country school building. He can plan for two paragraphs of comparison. One paragraph would begin, "George's school building is like my school building in many ways." The second paragraph would begin, "But in many other ways our school buildings are very different."

In other words, he could use this planning framework:

COMPARISON FRAMEWORK A

Name here the two things you are comparing.
They are alike in these ways: 1, 2, 3, etc.
They differ in these ways: 1, 2, 3, etc.

The other possibility goes like this. Timothy can list the characteristics on which he would like to compare the two buildings—

location, size, appearance, etc.—and jot down the details for each building next to each characteristic. In other words, he could use this framework:

COMPARISON FRAMEWORK B

	Name one of the subjects.	*Name the other subject.*
1. Characteristic being compared	Details about one subject	Details about other subject
2. Another characteristic	Details	Details
3.		
etc.		

Framework A is the better one to use when the two subjects being compared are alike on as many points as they are unlike. Framework B works better when the "ways alike" and "ways unlike" are very unbalanced—alike in three ways, unlike in one way, for example.

One of the writing assignments in chapter 1 called for a comparison of your school with schools shown in movies or on TV. As soon as Robert began thinking about that topic, he knew he would use Framework B because everything that came into his head was an "unlike."

So his writing plan came out like this:

	My school	**TV schools**
Student body	Great variety	Look alikes
Teachers	Some good, some bad	Extremes— heroes, villains
Principal	Ordinary guy	Extreme— superman or ridiculous
Activities	Routine	Excitement, special events

With the plan for the composition jotted down, the writer must decide what message he wants to get across about his two subjects. Robert had no trouble deciding that his message—his thesis statement or statement of purpose—would be "School, for me, is an ordinary place where ordinary people do routine things, but on TV every school day seems to be a special event."

By this time the relationship between a framework and a writing plan should be clear. You have seen that when the writing task is a narrative/experience, a piece of persuasive writing, or a comparison, there is a framework—a pattern—available for your use. You now understand that you simply look at the framework, fill it in with information concerning your subject, write your thesis statement—your message or writing purpose—and you have your writing plan.

There are two more kinds of writing for which there are built-in frameworks—business letters and book reports on novels. For each of these you will be given the framework and an example of a writing plan based on that framework. You will understand the relationship between them.

PRE-WRITING PLANNING
OF A BOOK REPORT

The planning framework for a book report on a novel looks like this:

FRAMEWORK FOR A
BOOK REPORT ON A NOVEL

Point to be covered	Details
Identification of book	Here you name the book and its author; identify what kind of novel it is—adventure study, mystery, romance, science fiction; tell the setting, that is, the locations where the action takes place; tell the time when the story takes place.
Characters	Here you name the main characters with a word or two for each to remind you what to tell your readers about them.
Plot	Here you tell what problem(s) the author creates for his characters and, without revealing the outcome, tell how the problems are handled.
Your opinion	Here you tell what you enjoyed/did not like about the book and whether you would/would not recommend it to your classmates.

Using the framework, Sally made this plan for her book report.

Superfudge by Judy Blume; story of family life; Manhattan and Princeton, NJ; present.
Farley Drexel Hatcher, the four-year-old "Fudge"; Peter, his fifth-grade brother; Tootsie, the new baby sister; their parents; friends Jimmy and Alex; girls in Peter's life—Sheila whom he can't stand and Joanne whom he finds himself liking, a lot.
Mr. Hatcher's decision to take a year off from his Manhattan advertising job to write a book takes the family to a new way of life, new school, new friends. Fudge's talent for getting into weird situations, plus the problems of adjusting to a new baby, keep things happening during a year that ends with an important family decision.
Liked the lively pace of the story and especially liked Peter, although he's almost too good to be true. If you like family stories, you'll like this one, even though Superfudge is a pain in the neck at times

A book report needs no thesis statement. The opinion section of the report expresses the writer's message.

PRE-WRITING PLANNING OF A BUSINESS LETTER

One of the writing tasks listed in chapter 1 was to write a letter to a retired business executive inviting her to visit a class to tell about her recent trip to Latin America. This, of course, would be a business letter.

There are rules about how a business letter must look, that is, about the form of the letter. When you write a letter to a friend or relative—a so-called friendly letter—it might look like this:

January 2, 19—

Dear Aunt Molly,

In the so-called body of the letter you tell her how much you liked your Christmas gift and you thank her for it.

You tell her that you hope you will see her soon. Then

Love,

Harry

It would not matter if you wrote "Tuesday afternoon" instead of the date; "Hi Aunt Molly" instead of "Dear Aunt Molly"; "Your favorite nephew" instead of "Love." But a business letter must look like a business letter. Here is one form that is frequently used:

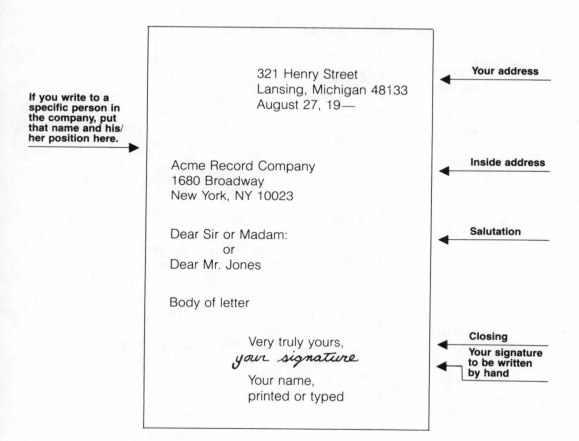

Your address

321 Henry Street
Lansing, Michigan 48133
August 27, 19—

If you write to a specific person in the company, put that name and his/her position here.

Acme Record Company
1680 Broadway
New York, NY 10023

Inside address

Dear Sir or Madam:
or
Dear Mr. Jones

Salutation

Body of letter

Very truly yours,

your signature

Closing

Your signature to be written by hand

Your name,
printed or typed

The body of a business letter, like any other piece of writing, must be planned. The planning is made easier because there is a framework that can be used for many of the letters that people write to carry on personal business. Such letters are likely to have one of these purposes: (1) to order something, (2) to complain about something, (3) to get information, or (4) to ask someone to do something for you. The letter that the class was asked to write is an example of the fourth purpose. So Victor used this business letter framework:

FRAMEWORK FOR A BUSINESS LETTER

Purpose of paragraph	Details	
1. Tell why writing	If ordering:	Identify advertisement or other source of information about product.
	If complaining:	State what object/service is being complained about
	If seeking information or If asking a favor:	State why information or favor is needed State why recipient was chosen as source of information or favor
2. Supply needed information	Give *all the facts* recipient will need to fill your order, or do something about your complaint, or supply the information you need, or do the favor you are asking for	
3. Sign off	If ordering. Tell how you are paying. If complaining. Tell what response you want to your complaint. If seeking information or a favor. State that you look forward to receiving the information receiving a favorable response concerning the favor.	

And he very easily made this writing plan:

Writing for Mr. B's sixth-grade class in
Centerville School

Doing unit on Latin America

Need current information

Saw report your trip, *Daily Argus,*
January 10, 19—

Visit on January 24 or February 6?

School location shown in address above

Class meets Room 220, 10:30, 40 minutes

Tell what you think most important for us to know about
Argentina, Chile, today

Time for us to ask questions

Look forward to answer

3

BUILDING WRITING PLANS FROM THE BOTTOM UP: Personal Compositions

In chapter 1 the term *personal compositions* was explained as writing in which the writer expresses feelings, emotions, reactions, or thoughts, the way he or she sees people or places; or his or her knowledge about something. The compositions are "personal" because the writer supplies personal raw material.

Pre-writing planning for these compositions is very different from the kind covered in the previous chapter.

START WITH JOTTINGS

Once you have decided that the writing task is a personal composition, your planning begins with jottings. Jottings are a kind of personal shorthand that people use all the time. Grace will jot down the word *keys* to remind herself to leave the extra set of car keys at Bill's office. Harriet jots down the word *keys* and later "reads" this message to herself: "Pick up the keys to the Youth Center at Town Hall." In the planning of a personal composition you jot down a list of words and phrases to remind yourself of whatever comes to your mind as you think about a topic—thoughts, feelings, memories, reactions, pieces of information—whatever is in your "mental attic."

This process of jotting down the thoughts triggered by a topic is a kind of "brainstorming." Groups of people sometimes engage in brainstorming sessions when they have a problem to solve and want to get out in the open all the ideas the members of the group can dredge up on the subject. The rules for such a brainstorming session are very explicit. No contribution is rejected; nobody argues about something that is put forward. And that's just the way you should approach the jotting process. Put down whatever comes to mind. Don't worry about whether the idea belongs on the list or not; don't worry about whether it's important or unimportant; don't try to do any organizing as you go. All that comes later.

Of course there is no such thing as a "right" jotting or a "wrong" jotting. And of course your jottings on a topic will look very different from other students' jottings on the same subject. For example, for a composition on the topic "The Empty House," here are three students' jottings:

Ann's list	*Bruce's list*	*Carl's list*
Sad	Strange noises	Windows—
Parties	Where people?	sunshine
Decorating	Place to play	Big enough for big
Backyard mailbox	Spooky lights	family
Lonesome	Place to explore	Backyard—trees
		Back from road

This jotting process is no big deal. You don't need many items. Five or six ideas about a topic can easily become a two- or three-paragraph composition. So the rough jotted notes go down quickly, and you move on to organizing them into a writing plan.

FINDING RELATIONSHIPS

First, the jottings are sorted into groups, each group containing only items that belong together. To put this another way: You must put into one group jottings that have something in common and put into a different group the jottings that have a different something-in-common, and in some cases into a third group the jottings that have a still different something-in-common.

Finding something-in-common relationships—ways in which things are alike—can be a very simple task or a very sophisticated task. The ability to see something-in-common relationships is well worth cultivating because that ability does much more than make you a better writer. Students who can see and express something-in-common relationships are not only better writers but better readers, better speakers, better test takers—just plain all-around better students.

There is no problem, of course, in identifying the something-in-common relationships in a list like this: apples, pears, spinach, beans, grapes, peas. Obviously apples, pears, and grapes have something in common: they are all fruits. Obviously spinach, beans, and peas have something in common: they are all vegetables.

But usually you must go through a mental question-and-answer process in order to identify a something-in-common relationship. For example, which piece of writing does not belong in this group: a prologue, a postscript, an introduction, a preface? You think this way: What's a prologue? beginning of a play; a postscript? something added after signing a letter; an introduction? something at the beginning of writing; a preface? something before the real part of the book gets started. And you decide: Prologue, introduction, and preface have something in common: they are all beginnings of writings. Postscript does not belong with them because it's something tacked onto the end of a piece of writing.

In the two examples above, you found something-in-common relationships in lists of words simply by asking yourself, about each item: What is this? You can use that process with this list too: skiing, ice skating, tennis racket, swimming, baseball bat, hockey stick. By asking "What is this?" about the six items, you can turn the unorganized list into an organized list like this, which shows the something-in-common relationships:

Sports
    skiing
    ice skating
    swimming

Things used for sports
    tennis racket
    baseball bat
    hockey stick

An organized list, you notice, groups items under *headings* that name the something-in-common of each group.

FROM JOTTINGS TO WRITING PLANS

When the items to be sorted are words and phrases jotted down in the planning of a personal composition, the writer goes through the same mental process but uses a different question. Each of the jotted items stands for an idea that went through the writer's head as he or she thought about the topic. So the question to be asked about each jotting is: What is this jotting *about*?

That question needs a little explaining. A good writer/reader/ student can understand the message of a sentence or a paragraph. But it is also necessary to be aware of what the sentence or paragraph is about. He or she must be able to think like this: Suppose the sentence reads, "The house is red." No question about the message. But what is the sentence about? The house, yes. Then comes another sentence, "The house is old." What is it about? The house. Then what's the difference between the first sentence and the second sentence? The first is about the appearance of the house; the second is about its age.

"Harry is tall." Message clear. What is it about? Harry, yes. But better, Harry's appearance, or how Harry looks, or Harry's physical characteristics. Then comes another sentence. "Harry is good-natured." What is the sentence about? Harry, yes. But better, Harry's disposition, or Harry's personality.

Why all this emphasis on "aboutness"? Because "aboutness" is the key to organization. Here is an example of how the question "What is this jotting about?" can be used to sort jottings.

When Ann saw the topic, "The Empty House," she thought of a real empty house, the house next door to her own. As you saw on page 27 she jotted down "sad, parties, decorating, backyard mailbox, lonesome." Ann knew the message of each of her jottings. She knew that when she jotted down "sad" it was to record the thought that "I'm sad about Jenny's family moving away." She wrote "parties" when she remembered the fun, in the now empty house, on birthdays and Halloween. "Decorating" was jotted down when she remembered good times fixing up Jenny's bedroom; "backyard mailbox" recorded the memory that "we used to write letters to each other and leave them in the tree in the backyard." "Lonesome" meant "Jenny was my best friend and I am lonesome without her."

So all Ann had to do to organize her jottings was to ask herself, for each jotting, "What is this about?" The answers came out like this:

Sad	is about	how I feel about the empty house.
Parties	is about	a good memory I have about the house.
Decorating	is about	a good memory I have about the house.
Backyard mailbox	is about	a good memory I have about the house.
Lonesome	is about	how I feel about the empty house.

Ann's writing plan, therefore, looked like this:

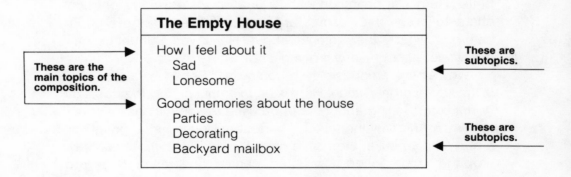

These are the main topics of the composition.

The Empty House

How I feel about it
    Sad
    Lonesome

Good memories about the house
    Parties
    Decorating
    Backyard mailbox

These are subtopics.

These are subtopics.

Try another example. In preparation for writing a composition on the topic "If Someone Left Me a Fortune," Gordon jotted down these ideas: buy computer, car—18, ice cream sodas, stereo in my room, money for college. He then took the first step in the process of turning his jottings into a composition writing plan. He asked himself, for each jotting, "What is this about?" The answers came out like this:

Buy computer   something I would do right now
Car—18   something I would put aside money for
Ice cream
    sodas   something I would buy right now
Stereo in my
    room   something I would buy right now
Money for
    college   something I would put money aside for

So his writing plan looked like this:

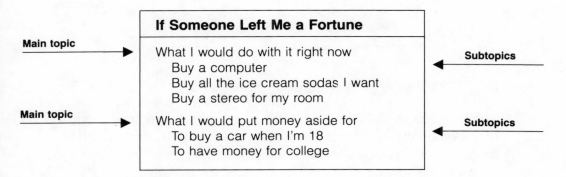

One more example: Harvey's sixth-grade class was asked to write a composition on this topic: "Guess Who This Is—a Description of Someone in Our Class." The rough notes for his writing plan looked like this:

Smaller than most other kids	how X looks
Full of wisecracks	how X acts
Gets in trouble a lot	how X acts
Dark brown hair never combed	how X looks
Likes to show off	how X acts

His writing plan looked like this:

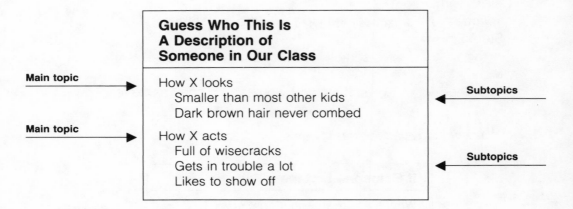

Main topic

Main topic

Subtopics

Subtopics

**Guess Who This Is
A Description of
Someone in Our Class**

How X looks
    Smaller than most other kids
    Dark brown hair never combed

How X acts
    Full of wisecracks
    Gets in trouble a lot
    Likes to show off

Suppose after you have grouped your jottings, you end up with an item that doesn't belong in any of your groups. When you label what it is about, you see that it has nothing in common with any of the other jottings on the list. Should the idea the jotting stands for go into the composition or should you just cross it out? Put it in, if (1) the idea is really related to the topic, and (2) it is an important idea, and (3) it does not change the mood or tone of the other ideas. If it does not meet these standards, drop it.

For example, Ann might have jotted down "white with green shutters" and labeled the jotting as being about "how the house looks." That is related to the topic, but is it as important as a group of ideas about Ann's feelings or a group of ideas about her memories? No, so it is better to drop the idea.

Harvey might have an orphan item like this, after sorting his jottings for the "Guess Who This Is" composition:

Basketball player   things X is good at

That is certainly on the topic and just as important in a description of X as his looks and his ways of behaving. What Harvey should do is try to think of more "things X is good at" and put them into the writing plan.

WRITING THESIS STATEMENTS

With the writing plan completed, the writer now prepares a sentence—as discussed in the preceding chapter—that states the purpose, the overall message, the thesis of the composition. As you now know, such a statement is easy to prepare because the writer has done all the thinking about what's going into the composition and what is being deliberately left out. It is a useful step because it forces the writer to decide on the tone and style he or she will try for in writing.

For example, Ann's thesis statement might go like this: "Every time I go past the empty house next door, remembering almost makes me cry." This will remind Ann to describe the good memories wistfully, in a style that says, "But it's all over now."

In contrast to Ann's approach to "The Empty House," Bruce's jottings, which you saw on page 27, suggest that he probably would come up with a thesis statement like this: "The empty house was fun for us in the daytime but we kept away from it at night." Carl's jottings look as if he was thinking of a real or imagined house that would make a great home for some family. So he would probably state his thesis like this: "When people stop to look at the empty house on the corner, it seems to call out, 'Come look at what a great home I would be.'"

Gordon's writing plan suggests that he takes a lighthearted but somewhat practical view of what he would do with a fortune, so his thesis statement might be: "If my rich uncle left me a fortune, I sure would have a ball, but I think I'd have sense enough not to act as if there is no tomorrow."

Harvey obviously wants to tell the truth in his description of X, but X is his friend so he states his message as: "You would never pick X out as the biggest or the neatest sixth grader in town, but if he's around for a while, you'll notice him."

Now we move on to applying the process described in this chapter to research reports.

4
WRITING PLANS FOR RESEARCH REPORTS

Chapter 1 included two examples of assignments that require "personal compositions to inform." In one assignment a list of topics was given—computer games, the scientific method, the guidance program in your school—and you were told to choose one that you know something about. The other assignment was to tell someone your own age how to do something or make something that you know how to do or make.

The writing plan for either of these compositions would be made using the process explained in the preceding chapter. You would jot down a list to remind you of the pieces of information you want to give your readers. Then you would organize those jottings according to what they are about. The organized list would be your writing plan.

A research report is a special kind of personal composition to inform. You supply the raw material, but that raw material is not information that is in your head right now, information that you have picked up over the years in a variety of ways. The raw material for a research paper is gathered by reading or by interviewing people, usually the former.

To make all of this clearer, here is an account of how sixth-grade Elaine made the writing plan for her research report.

CHOOSING AN APPROPRIATE TOPIC

Elaine's teacher made this assignment:

> *Our next social studies unit will deal with India. During the last week of our study of India you are to hand in a research report on a topic related to one of the following:*
>> *Industry in India*
>> *Farming in India*
>> *Religions of India*
>> *Art of India*

Notice that the assignment calls for a report on a topic *related to* one of the above. Each of the four areas listed is much too broad to be covered in an interesting way in the two- or three-page report that is usually expected from you at this school level.

Research reports can be interesting, interesting to do and interesting to read, but they can also be extremely dull for both writer and audience. The interesting ones have lots of details, behind-the-scenes information, anecdotes. You can only include that kind of material and still cover your topic, if the topic is of reasonable size.

So the first task in a research/report assignment is usually to identify an appropriately narrow topic. An encyclopedia is an extremely useful tool for doing just that. An encyclopedia article on any subject is a comprehensive overview of that subject. In that overview you will find mention of incidents, places, and people that sound as if, pursued further in more specialized sources, they would interest you, your classmates, and your teacher.

Elaine read the "Farming" section of an encyclopedia article on India and saw some information that helped her to decide on this topic: "How Farming Is Changing in Some Indian Villages." She then did this work in the library:

- She found appropriate sources of information on her small topic and prepared bibliography cards for those she actually used.
- She took notes on information related to her topic, keying each note card to the source in which she found it.

This book does not cover how to do the two tasks listed above, so if you do not know exactly how to do them you might want to look at *How to Write a Report*, by Gerald Newman (New York: Franklin Watts, 1980).

When Elaine was finished with her library work she had eleven note cards, which are reproduced on pages 39–40. Her four bibliography cards, numbered 1–4 are not shown, but the number in a circle on each note card tells which of the four sources that note came from.

FROM NOTE CARDS
TO WRITING PLAN

With her note cards completed, Elaine is at the point where Ann, Gordon, and Harvey were when they finished jotting down words and phrases suggested by a topic. Their jottings are the raw material for a composition; Elaine's note cards are the raw material for a research report. They had to organize their jottings into a writing plan; Elaine must organize her note cards into a writing plan. They grouped together the jottings that had something in common; Elaine must group together the cards that have something in common. They found the something-in-common by considering what each jotting was about; Elaine will find the something-in-common by considering what each card is about.

Elaine's task might seem more difficult because she has eleven note cards, while Ann, Gordon, and Harvey had fewer than half that number of jottings. Furthermore, each card has a goodly number of words on it; the jottings were very brief.

What makes sorting note cards easy, however, is that they can be physically shuffled around until you have two or three or four little piles of cards. You don't stop shuffling until you can go through the cards in each pile and say: "This one is about...; and so is this one; and so is this one. They are all about..."

Shuffling Elaine's note cards produced these two piles:

- A pile about problems that make changes necessary.

  Cards B, C, G, H, J were in this pile.

- A pile about the kinds of changes that are being made to meet farming problems.

  Cards A, E, I, K were in this pile.

A

Control of erosion ①

    Dikes being built on fields —
stop erosion during monsoon

B

Poverty of small farmer ②

    Farmers with small farms
can't afford:

    fertilizer, tractors, tube wells,
pumps

C

Inadequate irrigation ②

    Only 20% of India's
farmland is irrigated;
35 - 50% could be.

D

Land unfairly divided. ②

    Land reform needed —

    Farmland must be divided so
all can have jobs on land —
No room in cities for more
people

E

Improved irrigation ③

    Recent irrigation schemes,
dams, tube wells decrease
dependence upon monsoon

F

Land shortage   ③

Biggest problem is too little land to feed huge population

G

Monsoon   ③

big problem

Its prompt arrival, proper distribution, and quantity make difference between food security or famine

H

Land shortage   ①

Forces some to farm on hills — here farmers depend completely on monsoon for water

I

New machinery   ④

Tractors, mechanical threshers, other machinery used mostly by large farmers — over 10 acres

J

Shortage of machinery   ④

Supply of farm machinery less than demand

India produced 30,000 tractors in 1970
Had to import 15,000 more

K

Improved seeds   ③

Improved seeds and improved fertilizers increase amount land can produce

Cards D, F, and J turned out to be orphan cards. Card D is about a proposal for land reform to make things better in the future, but Elaine's topic is limited to things going on right now, so she discarded Card D. Cards F and J state problems, but Elaine found no suggestions for remedies, so she dropped them.

A SPECIAL KIND OF
WRITING PLAN—AN OUTLINE

The writing plan for a research report is usually a formal outline. Such an outline can easily be constructed. The something-in-common for each pile of cards becomes a main topic. The cards in each pile, arranged in the order that makes the best sense, become the subtopics. Here is how Elaine's outline came out. We have put in parentheses after each subtopic the note card on which it is based.

How Farming Is Changing in Some Indian Villages

I. *Problems that make changes necessary*
   A. *Dependence on monsoon (G)*
   B. *Inadequate irrigation*
      1. *Percentage of land irrigated (C)*
      2. *Why some is not irrigated (H)*
   C. *Effect of poverty on farming (B)*

II. *Kinds of changes being made to meet problems*
   A. *Control of erosion (A)*
   B. *New ways of irrigation (E)*
   C. *Use of machinery on larger farms (I)*
   D. *Improved seeds and fertilizers (K)*

THE THESIS STATEMENT

The thesis statement for a research report must define exactly what the report covers. The thinking that went into Elaine's outline made it easy for her to write such a statement, thus: In many villages in India, new ways of farming are helping with some old problems.

Chapters 2, 3, and 4 have described the planning that precedes many kinds of writing. The chapters that follow will show how smoothly first drafts emerge from pre-writing plans. Actually, at this point the writing of the first draft has already begun, for thesis statements are the openings, or appear close to the openings, of most writing.

5

WRITING THE FIRST DRAFT: Good Beginnings— Good Endings

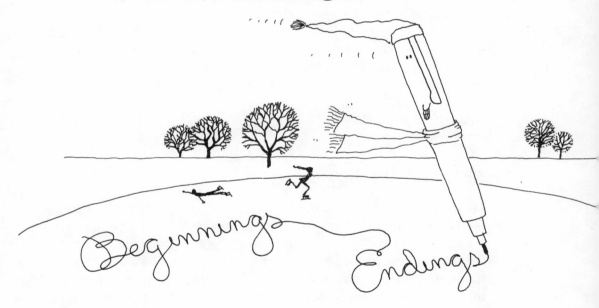

Nobody can go directly from a writing plan to a finished composition—nobody, that is, who wants to produce the best composition of which he or she is capable. The first paper you write is a draft. It's going to be changed.

Let's get out of the way at the outset four recommendations concerning the mechanics of writing the first draft of your composition.

- Write the first draft on different paper from that to be used for final copy.

- Write on every other line, not every line, so there will be room for editing changes.

- If, as you write, you decide to make changes, don't erase. Cross out, make the change, and move on.

- If you are not sure about some matters of mechanics—spelling, capitalization, punctuation—circle the trouble spot and move along. This is not dictionary time or ask-teacher time.

Now, down to business.

ABOUT BEGINNINGS

The first words of the first draft are governed by probably the most basic rule of writing: Every piece of writing must have a beginning, a middle, and an ending. That seems like such obvious common sense that one might say: Nobody needs a rule like that. Writing that way is simply "doing what comes naturally." And, to a degree, that is true. But in the writing you do in school, appropriate beginnings and endings rarely come naturally.

Arthur, for example, writing an assigned composition, thinks he is following the rule when he goes at a composition this way. He opens his composition with this sentence: "I am going to tell you about how air bags work in automobiles." Then he describes what air bags look like, where they are placed in cars, what triggers their inflation, how they protect passengers. He ends his composition with this sentence: "That is how air bags work." Arthur's first and last sentences may follow the letter of the rule but they certainly do not follow the spirit of the rule.

Think about the speakers who have appeared in your school assemblies, the talks you have heard in your place of worship. How often have they begun with a story, a joke—something to get you listening? The speakers usually follow the story or joke with a few words about why they told it, and in this explanation they announce what they are going to talk about and then go into the "middle," the substance of the speech. If they are good speakers, they spend the last minute or so pulling together what they have said, trying to leave you with a big idea to carry away.

What good speakers do, good writers do. Needless to say, in the short pieces of writing you are asked to do at this stage in school there isn't room for a story at the beginning and a summary wrap-up at the end. But you must still try for a beginning that attracts the reader's attention; you must still try to sign off, not just stop.

By this time you probably realize that you already know one good kind of beginning—thesis statements. And they *are* appropriate beginnings for brief writing pieces if they have some flavor of originality about them.

How would the thesis statements we have made so far serve as beginnings?

Watching a ballet rehearsal helps a ballet-goer understand how wonderful performances are created.	You might want to precede it with something like: "I am a real ballet fan. Last week I saw my first ballet rehearsal, and let me tell you that watching a ballet rehearsal..." But the thesis statement itself would be a better first sentence than many student papers achieve.

School, for me, is an ordinary place where ordinary people do routine things, but on TV every school day seems to be a special event.

Again, you might precede this with something like: "TV school movies make me laugh. School, for me..." But again, the thesis statement could open the composition.

Every time I go past the empty house next door, remembering almost makes me cry.

An adequate opening sentence that could be dressed up by preceding it with something like: "I don't know how you feel about empty houses, but every time I go..."

If my rich uncle left me a fortune I sure would have a ball, but I think I'd have sense enough not to act as if there is no tomorrow.

This would be an acceptable opening sentence, or it could be jazzed up like this: "I have a rich uncle. I really do. And if my..."

You would never pick X out as the biggest or the neatest sixth grader in town, but if he's around for a while, you'll notice him.

We happen to be very fond of this thesis sentence and would leave it entirely alone as the first sentence of the composition.

Did you notice that the additional words suggested as beginnings have something in common? They all refer directly to the reader or the writer; that kind of reference is one, simple attention-getting device.

The beginning of a research report must be more than the thesis statement. In the first place, there is room for more. It is the longest of the writing pieces we have worked with. More important, the thesis statement of a research report is—as it must be—very down-to-earth, too much so to accomplish what the beginning is supposed to do, namely, get the reader's attention.

As Elaine did her research she was on the lookout for a story she could use as a beginning. She found mention of farmers who were reluctant to try new seeds that, on other farms, had greatly increased crops. The farmers were afraid the seeds might not work and they would have no crops at all. Elaine made up her own little story and began her composition this way:

> Raj was sorry that the man in the white coat was so disappointed.
> "These seeds will give you bigger crops," he had said.
> "But suppose they do not grow," Raj had replied. "I have used the old seeds all my life, and we have always had something to eat even if it wasn't always enough. I am afraid to change."
> The man in the white coat had left and gone on to the next farm, where Kami said yes to the offer of seeds.
> Many Indian farmers think like Raj, but a growing number think like Kami and in many Indian villages...

OTHER KINDS OF BEGINNINGS

The beginning of any persuasive paper you are asked to write can be one sentence that leads into your opinion statement. This was the writing plan for a letter to the editor of the "Our Readers Write Us" column of the school newspaper.

Larry's Writing Plan

The Board of Education should provide funds for the school to buy additional clothing lockers.	
1. Number of students vs. number of hall lockers	600 students, 450 lockers Some broken locks Some rusty doors
2. Students wearing outdoor clothing inside	Health Appearance Arguments with teachers
3. Students allowed to use closets in classrooms	Interrupted classes Teachers with keys not around

This composition could begin:

Dear Editor:

There is a serious problem in our school that needs attention—shortage of clothing lockers. I think that the...

It is accepted practice that the first sentence(s) of a book report should give the reader the information in the first box of the writing plan. So Sally's book report would open with a sentence like this:

"*Superfudge* is a story of present-day family life. The action takes place in the Manhattan apartment and Princeton house where the Hatcher family live and in the school and other neighborhood places to which their daily activities take them."

First Part of Sally's Writing Plan

Superfudge by Judy Blume;

story of family life;

Manhattan and Princeton, NJ;

present

The beginning of a business letter should give the reason for writing. Thus, the first paragraph of Victor's letter to Ms. Jaspar should go like this:

Dear Ms. Jaspar:

I am writing to you as a representative of Mr. Bennett's sixth-grade class in Centerville School. We are doing a unit on Latin America and need information about current conditions there. We were very much interested, therefore, to read in the Daily Argus *of January 10, 19— that you recently returned from a trip to Argentina and Chile.*

First Part of Victor's Writing Plan

Details
Writing for Mr. B's sixth grade class in Centerville School
Doing unit on Latin America
Need current information
Saw report your trip, *Daily Argus,* January 10, 19—

ENDINGS

This was said before, but it bears repeating: a writer must sign off, not just stop. One way to be sure you have a real ending for your composition is to write it at the same time you write the beginning. This makes sense because, with two exceptions, the ending is built from the beginning. A book report ends with your opinion and recommendation; a business letter ends as shown in the framework. With these exceptions, the final sentence(s) of a brief composition

- rephrase the opening sentences, or
- raise a question or make an observation clearly related to the opening sentence(s).

To test your understanding of this principle, here is a list of seven pieces of writing that have been worked with in this and other chapters:

1. Ann's personal composition about the empty house
2. Larry's letter to the column editor about lockers
3. Harvey's personal composition describing someone he likes
4. Gordon's personal composition about what he would do if he suddenly acquired a lot of money
5. Robert's comparison of a real place with places shown on TV
6. Mary's personal composition about an experience in a theater
7. Elaine's research report

And here is a list of seven "ending" sentences. Choose the appropriate ending for each of the seven pieces of writing listed above. That will be easy, of course. But after you make each choice, ask yourself: Why is this a good ending for that composition? Better yet, see if you can come up with an ending for that composition that you think would work better.

A. "I hope your readers will support my position."
B. "Uncle Alex, if you leave me your fortune, I will thank you now, and on and on and on."
C. "I wonder if it will ever be a happy house again."
D. "This glimpse of what goes on behind the scenes is going to make real performances more exciting than ever."
E. "If the pockets of farming progress now seen here and there in India spread, a brighter future for India seems to lie ahead."
F. "But here's the most important thing I have to tell you about X. He's my friend."
G. "With all that excitement in TV schools, how do you suppose those kids do on their SATs?"

6

WRITING THE FIRST DRAFT: Good Middles

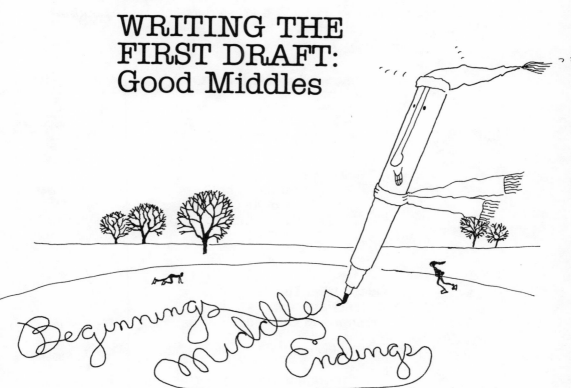

The middle of any piece of writing is the writer's biggest task. It is the substance of the piece, and it must be written with two purposes in mind: (1) to communicate and (2) to interest. Communicating effectively is largely a matter of organization; writing interestingly is largely a matter of style.

FROM PLANS
TO PARAGRAPHS

The writing plans reproduced here will ensure well-organized compositions if they are faithfully translated into sentences and paragraphs.

If Someone Left Me a Fortune

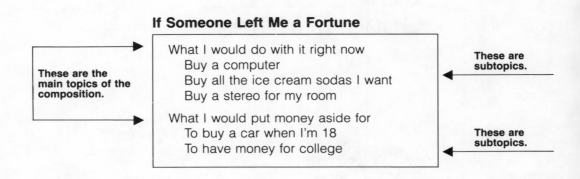

These are the main topics of the composition.

What I would do with it right now
    Buy a computer
    Buy all the ice cream sodas I want
    Buy a stereo for my room

What I would put money aside for
    To buy a car when I'm 18
    To have money for college

These are subtopics.

These are subtopics.

Guess Who This Is
A Description of
Someone in Our Class

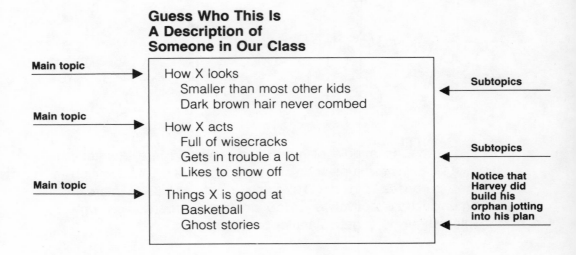

Main topic

Main topic

Main topic

How X looks
    Smaller than most other kids
    Dark brown hair never combed

How X acts
    Full of wisecracks
    Gets in trouble a lot
    Likes to show off

Things X is good at
    Basketball
    Ghost stories

Subtopics

Subtopics

Notice that Harvey did build his orphan jotting into his plan

The Empty House

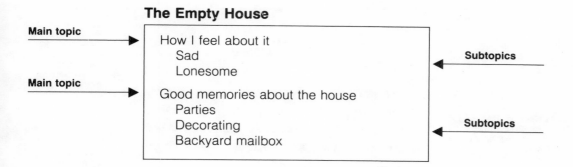

Main topic →

How I feel about it
   Sad
   Lonesome

← **Subtopics**

Main topic →

Good memories about the house
   Parties
   Decorating
   Backyard mailbox

← **Subtopics**

Each main topic on these writing plans becomes the topic sentence of a paragraph. At this point in your writing career the topic sentence is usually placed at the beginning of the paragraph, but you may put it at the end if it works better. The paragraph is developed from the subtopics. Each subtopic is turned into at least one sentence; some may need two or three sentences.

Subtopics need not be written into the paragraph in the sequence shown on the plan. When you come to a topic that has more than two subtopics, stop a minute and decide on the best sequence in which to present the details. One good way to sequence them is to put the best—most interesting detail, strongest reason—last.

When you are a more experienced writer, doing lengthier pieces, you will write many paragraphs with no topic sentence and some with the topic sentence in the middle of the paragraph. That is perfectly all right as long as all of the sentences in the paragraph are about the same topic. But for the present, to be sure your organization is clear and clean, write a topic sentence for each paragraph, taking it from your writing plan, and develop the paragraph with your details, taking them from your writing plan.

As an example of the process described above, here is one way Ann could turn her writing plan into a composition.

The Empty House

Notice that Ann decided to dress up her thesis statement for her beginning.

I don't know how you feel about empty houses, but every time I go past the empty house next door, remembering almost makes me cry. ▲ *I have so many unhappy feelings now about that house. Jenny lived there, and Jenny was my best friend from kindergarten days. Off to California the family went, and that makes me sad. I'm lonesome too. I know lots of kids, but they're not real friends, around all the time.*

Here is the topic sentence made from the first main topic.

Here are the subtopics made into sentences.

No topic sentence; she must be planning to put it at the end.

That big tree in the backyard has a branch that's just right for holding things. It was our special mailbox for the long letters we wrote to each other even after spending the whole afternoon together. We could spend hours on anything. Finding a place for Jenny's new chair took us days of furniture moving. Making new curtains to go with the chair kept us busy for weeks. How many parties I have gone to in that house! Birthdays, Halloween, last-day-of-school were all party days. If there was no holiday to celebrate, we made up a reason for friends and food and music. There are plenty of happy memories in that empty house. I wonder if it will ever be a happy house again.

See the subtopics?

Here's the topic sentence.

Good place for it because it leads right into the ending sentence.

FROM FRAMEWORK
WRITING PLANS
TO PARAGRAPHS

The framework writing plans developed in Chapter 2 become composition middles as readily as the writing plans developed from the bottom up, from jottings. Take, for example, the writing plan that Mary made for her personal experience composition. Each scene in an experience framework becomes a paragraph. Each scene setting is turned into a topic sentence, like this:

1. Lobby of theater—
visitors being prepared
to watch rehearsal

"My rehearsal experience began in the lobby of the theater, where the invited group assembled to be prepared for what lay ahead."

2. In balcony of theater,
waiting for rehearsal to
start

"Grateful to have gotten into our seats without breaking our necks, we glued our eyes to the stage, watching the dancers as they waited for the rehearsal to begin."

Then, again, details turned into sentences to develop the paragraph.

3. Watching dancers at
work

"Once the rehearsal started, there was so much to watch that we could hardly take it all in."

Again, details used to develop the paragraph.

Here is the framework writing plan that Larry made for his persuasive composition, his letter to the "Our Readers Write Us" column:

The Board of Education should provide funds for the school to buy additional clothing lockers.	
1. Number of students vs. number of hall lockers	600 students, 450 lockers Some broken locks Some rusty doors
2. Students wearing outdoor clothing inside	Health Appearance Arguments with teachers
3. Students allowed to use closets in classrooms	Interrupted classes Teachers with keys not around

Each reason in a persuasive framework writing plan is turned into a sentence, which in turn becomes the topic sentence of a paragraph. Thus:

For reason 1   *There simply are not enough lockers in the halls, in decent condition, for the number of students in this school.*

For reason 2   *One result of the inadequate locker situation is that many students are wearing their outdoor clothing indoors.*

For reason 3   *To ease the locker situation, some teachers are allowing students to store their outdoor clothing in the closets inside the classrooms.*

Then the details related to each reason are turned into sentences to develop the paragraph.

Here is the framework writing plan for Victor's comparison composition:

	My school	*TV schools*
Student body	Great variety	Look alikes
Teachers	Some good, some bad	Extremes — heros, villains
Principal	Ordinary guy	Extreme— superman or ridiculous
Activities	Routine	Excitement, special events

Each characteristic being compared is the basis for a paragraph. However, if two or more characteristics have something in common, they may be combined in one paragraph. "Teachers" and "principal," for example, may be combined under "faculty."

The topic sentence of each paragraph names the characteristic and states whether the subjects being compared are alike or unlike in regard to that characteristic. Thus:

For the first characteristic	*TV students are certainly not like those in my school.*
For the second and third characteristics, combined under "faculty"	*Our faculty wouldn't last a week in any TV school I've seen, and most TV teachers and principals wouldn't last a day in our school.*

| For the last characteristic | *A typical school day on TV has nothing whatsoever to do with my school day.* |

As in the preceding framework writing plans, the details are then turned into sentences to develop each paragraph.

Framework writing plans for book reports are easy to turn into compositions. As explained in chapter 5, Sally had no problem writing her beginning straight out of her first box.

Superfudge by Judy Blume; story of family life; Manhattan and Princeton, NJ; present.
Farley Drexel Hatcher, the four-year-old "Fudge"; Peter, his fifth-grade brother; Tootsie, the new baby sister; their parents; friends Jimmy and Alex; girls in Peter's life—Sheila whom he can't stand and Joanne whom he finds himself liking, a lot.
Mr. Hatcher's decision to take a year off from his Manhattan advertising job to write a book takes the family to a new way of life, new school, new friends. Fudge's talent for getting into weird situations, plus the problems of adjusting to a new baby, keep things happening during a year that ends with an important family decision.
Liked the lively pace of the story and especially liked Peter, although he's almost too good to be true. If you like family stories, you'll like this one, even though Superfudge is a pain in the neck at times.

The box devoted to characters becomes the second paragraph of a book report. The topic sentence should state how the writer feels about the characters. Sally's topic sentence for the second paragraph might be "Some of the characters in this book seem more real than others, and certainly some are more likeable than others."

She would then develop the details on her writing plan into sentences that illustrate the point made in her topic sentence.

Similarly, the topic sentence for the paragraph about the plot should express how you feel about the plot. Sally's third paragraph might begin this way: "There is no big crisis or problem in the Hatcher family's year in Princeton, just a series of little crises and little problems, all of which end happily."

The final paragraph, dealing with your opinions about the book, opens with a topic sentence stating your opinion about the book as a whole or your recommendation about it to your classmates. Sally started her final paragraph this way: "I liked *Superfudge* because I like family stories full of little details about everyday life, even when the people are more thoughtful and loving than most of the families I know and even though everything works out for the best in a way that things don't always really work out."

Now here is Victor's framework writing plan for a business letter.

1. Reason for writing	Writing for Mr. B's sixth-grade class in Centerville School
	Doing unit on Latin America
	Need current information
	Saw report your trip, *Daily Argus,* January 10
2. Needed information	Visit on January 24 or February 6?
	School location shown in address above
	Class meets Room 220, 10:30, 40 minutes
	Tell what you think most important for us to know about Argentina, Chile today
	Time for us to ask questions
3. Sign off	Look forward to answer

The plan makes clear that there is no problem about division into paragraphs. It is equally clear that each paragraph can be developed with the details shown. There are no topic sentences in brief business letters such as this. (The long letters that businesspeople write are really "compositions" set in the business letter form, so they are planned and written using the processes that have been set forth for those kinds of writing.)

WAYS TO MAKE THE FIRST DRAFT INTERESTING

There are a number of ways to make compositions interesting. Perhaps you can figure out two of those ways for yourself by comparing two compositions on the same subject.

On page 56, you read Ann's composition, "The Empty House." We will pretend that another girl, Felicia, wrote a composition on the same topic. She used Ann's writing plan, Ann's beginning, Ann's first topic sentence, and Ann's ending. Here is her composition. As you read it, see if you are aware of important differences between it and Ann's.

The Empty House

I don't know how you feel about empty houses but every time I go past the empty house next door, remembering almost makes me cry. I have so many unhappy feelings now about that house. The family that lived there moved away. Jenny lived there. She was my friend for a long time. I'm sad that she moved. I'm lonesome too. The kids I know are not my friends.

*We put letters in a tree. We spent a lot
of time fixing Jenny's room. She got a new
chair. We found a place for it. We made
new curtains. We had lots of parties. We
had birthday parties and Halloween
parties. I remember good times in the
house. I wonder if it will ever be a happy
house again.*

It may help you to see why Ann's composition is more interesting than Felicia's if you think about these two points:

- Ann's has many more specific details. How many details can you find in Ann's composition that are missing from Felicia's?

- Its sentences are written in a variety of ways. Many sentences follow the pattern that students find easiest to write, that is, the subject of the sentence starts it off and the verb follows. But enough sentences start out differently to keep the composition from sounding *clunk-clunk-clunk*, as Felicia's composition sounds. For example, here are two sentences in which Ann put words giving "where" and "why" information before the subject:

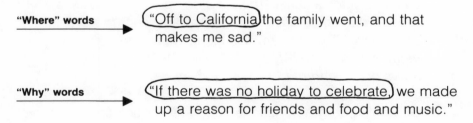

"Where" words ➤ "Off to California the family went, and that makes me sad."

"Why" words ➤ "If there was no holiday to celebrate, we made up a reason for friends and food and music."

Here are two sentences in which Ann used a phrase for the subject instead of a noun or a pronoun:

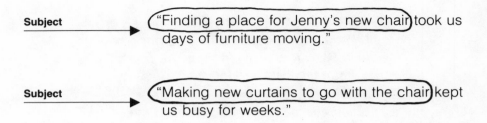

Subject   "Finding a place for Jenny's new chair took us days of furniture moving."

Subject   "Making new curtains to go with the chair kept us busy for weeks."

She even included one example of the kind of sentence that uses an exclamation point at the end instead of a period or question mark, that is, a sentence expressing strong feeling or excitement.

"How many parties I have gone to in that house!"

Gordon's composition about inheriting a fortune suggests other ways to make writing interesting. Here is his first paragraph:

If my rich uncle left me a fortune, I sure would have a ball, but I think I'd have sense enough not to act as if there is no tomorrow. The day I really have part of that fortune I'll start off on a spending spree. Every time I have just enough money for one ice cream soda and that rich, chocolaty syrup slides down my throat, I think what it would be like if this could go on and on. So the first money I spend will be to find out what one soda after another tastes like. Then I'll start on the big-ticket items. There's a computer in Hobson's window that takes dozens of games and can do word processing. That's on my list, along with a stereo set for my room. No more "TURN THAT THING OFF!" when I enjoy hours of my kind of big-sound music.

Gordon's paragraph has the varied sentences and fullness of detail that Ann's composition has, plus two other characteristics that contribute to an interesting style:

- He used vivid description words like "rich, chocolaty syrup," "big-sound music," "big-ticket items."
- He wrote for his audience, his classmates and teacher. He wrote as he would talk to them, and that is good in an informal composition. He would not write that way in a letter to the rich and stodgy uncle from whom he hopes to inherit the fortune.

More about choice of words: Mary's composition about the ballet rehearsal will try to make the reader live the experience by using phrases like "the dark cavern of the theater"; "fear of getting chilled revealed by their bulky leg warmers, yards of scarves, and layers of shirts and sweaters"; "bending and stretching like Olympic athletes"; "a leap that looked as if he were suspended in midair." Picture-making words like these make compositions interesting.

A personal composition that describes a person, place, or thing is more interesting when the writer not only makes you see what he is describing but also reveals how he feels about the subject. For example, Harvey included these two sentences in his "Guess Who This Is" personal composition:

Some people might say X's hair is messy, but I think he likes to look casual.

Nine kids can walk down the hall without a pass and not get caught. If X follows them, the principal will nab him.

Can you see how Harvey's choice of words shows that he thinks X's hair looks okay even though other people don't like the un-combed look? Can you see that his choice of words shows that he sympathizes with X's bad luck? He doesn't criticize him as a rule-breaker.

Another example: In describing a room you can write:

There are many family photographs in the room.

or,

The room is cluttered with family photographs.

or,

The room is made homelike by many family photographs.

Which sentence tells nothing of how the writer feels about the room? Which shows that the writer likes it? Which shows that the writer thinks the room is not pleasing?

In other kinds of writing, the writer pays special attention to other qualities of style. In persuasive writing, the writer tries for a forceful style. In a nominating speech, for example, the writer/ speaker would use phrases like "outstanding job," "tireless worker," "highly successful," "exceptionally well qualified." In the attempt to be forceful, however, the writer must still keep the audience in mind. Peter, for example, was asked to write a persuasive letter to his principal about the school lunch program. In it he dismissed school food with the judgment that "it stinks." Forceful, yes, but not appropriate style for the assigned task.

In research reports the writer works especially hard to be clear. He is careful to use words that show the relationship of ideas. In Elaine's research report, for example, she wrote:

Farmers who have no way to irrigate their crops must depend on the monsoon for water. If the monsoon begins when expected and lasts a normal length of time, all is well. But, if the monsoon...

Throughout her paper Elaine used words to signal contrast (like the word *but* above); others to show that she was giving a series of like things (*in addition*, *furthermore*, *second*, *etc.*). She made time relationships clear with words like *then*, *previously*, *meanwhile*, *at the same time*.

At last, there it is on your desk—a composition with a good beginning, a well-organized and interestingly written middle, and a good ending. But your work is far from over.

Chapter 7

FROM WRITER TO EDITOR

With the first draft completed, you drop the role of writer and take on the role of editor. This editorial role is so important to successful writing that you are often asked to hand in your first draft as well as the final paper. This is done when your teacher, or other evaluators, want to determine whether you do indeed know how to edit.

In the role of editor *you* judge your writing, so it is a good idea for you to know the basis on which *others* will evaluate it. There are dozens of checklists for evaluating writing, but they boil down to these basic questions:

Four about content:

1. Does the content of the writing piece accomplish what the topic and your statement of purpose—your thesis statement—promise?
2. Is the content interesting?
3. Does the content reveal originality and imagination?
4. Have you given enough details to support each of your main ideas adequately and appropriately?

Two about organization:

5. Is the writing piece well organized?
6. Have you used transition words to show how one idea is related to another?

Two about writing style:

7. Are the sentences free from sentence errors (run-on sentences and sentence fragments) and varied rather than all in a first-subject-then-verb sequence?
8. Is the language clear, specific, and colorful?

Questions related to editing for mechanics will be covered in the final chapter.

If you follow the revision procedures suggested in this chapter you will go a long way toward ensuring a yes answer to most of those questions.

FIRST STEP IN REVISION—
READING ALOUD

Revision begins this way: You read your first draft aloud. *Repeat: You read your first draft aloud.* Reading aloud goes more slowly than reading silently, so during the oral reading you are very likely to catch two specific kinds of errors that you would be almost certain to miss reading silently. Here are some examples of what happens during the reading-aloud process.

Patricia was reading aloud the part of her persuasive composition in which she argued against a change in the school lunchroom:

> *Why should we change it there's nothing wrong with the one we have now.*

She stopped after these words because she realized that she had not *read* it the way she *wrote* it. In reading, she had paused after the word *it* because it made sense to pause there. In other words, by reading aloud she had found a run-on sentence. "Why should we change it" is a complete thought. "There's nothing wrong with the one we have now" is a complete thought. She made the necessary revision this way:

> *Why should we change it there's nothing wrong with the one we have now.*

The three little lines under the *t* will remind her to make it a capital *T* when she writes the final copy. Reading aloud also shows up sentence fragments, that is, groups of words that do not carry a complete thought.

As David read aloud his lunchroom composition he came to this sentence:

I think it is a good idea to give us students a change to
decide whether we should change the lunchroom.

He stopped, realizing that he had *read* "give us a *chance*" even though he had written "give us a *change*." He made the necessary revision by crossing out "change" and writing "chance" above it. If you think that David is the only one who found he had not written what he meant to write, consider these excerpts from other compositions on the same topic:

a choice of soda, fish, and meat sandwiches, not evening
thinking about the french fries.
I don't why they are asking us.
It gives students time to eat want we want.

Can you see in each case what the writer meant to write? All of these errors can, of course, be easily fixed.

Reading aloud also helps you check up on the content of a piece of writing. For example, as Beatrice read aloud her lunchroom composition, she was surprised to hear herself say "throwing away" three times. She realized what she must check: Do I have only one reason for asking for a lunchroom change? Is waste of food the only point I've talked about? When Beatrice thinks up another reason, she writes a sentence or two about it. If there is room to fit it in on one of the lines she left blank she makes this sign (∧) where the new words are to go and writes them in. If there is not enough room, she can write them at the bottom of her first draft paper, label the new material "Insert A," and show where the insert belongs in the composition by doing this (^{Insert A}) in the
∧
appropriate place.

Students who make writing plans and translate them into first drafts in the ways we have suggested will not have serious content or organization problems. But just to be sure, after the reading aloud, ask yourself questions 1 and 4. Be especially diligent to root out any wandering-off words not justified by your plan.

SILENT READING FOR TRANSITIONS

As a final check on content and organization read your work silently and look for sentences that need to be linked in some way in order to clarify the message. In other words, insert transitional words where they are needed. This came up in connection with Elaine's research report, but the subject is important enough to go over again.

Consider this example. Suppose you have written:

On the day set for the picnic the rain came down in sheets. All our plans were ruined.

The second sentence is a logical follow-up of the first; no transition word is needed. On the other hand, suppose you have written:

On the day set for the picnic the rain came down in sheets. We had a great time.

There the second sentence has an unexpected relationship to the preceding sentence. You must signal the unexpected by a transition word so the reader won't be thrown off the track. *Nevertheless* would be an appropriate signal word here, or even *but*.

Don't give up on the transitions checkup until you are sure you have given your reader all the help he or she needs with time sequence, cause-effect sequences, and other idea relationships.

SILENT READING
FOR SENTENCE QUALITY

In the preceding chapter we pretended that a girl named Felicia wrote a composition on the same topic that Ann used, "The Empty House."

She used Ann's writing plan, her beginning, her first topic sentence, and her ending. But in the middle her sentences clunked along like this:

> *We put letters in a tree. We spent a lot of time fixing Jenny's room. She got a new chair. We found a place for it. We made new curtains.*

You certainly do not want your composition to sound like that. So, read your composition again, silently. Lightly underline the first three or four words of each sentence. Are you clunking along with all first-subject-then-verb sentences?

If you decide you have insufficient sentence variety, here are some easy ways to make changes.

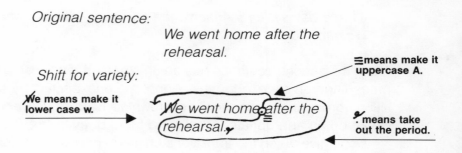

Original sentence:
We went home after the rehearsal.

Shift for variety:

≡means make it uppercase A.

We means make it lower case w.

We went home after the rehearsal.

. means take out the period.

In other words, it is often possible to shift words that tell the "when" of a sentence.

Original sentence:

The stagehands worked right next to the dancers.

Marked for revision:

Ignoring the dancers leaping at their backs, ^The stagehands ~~worked right next to the~~ moved props and adjusted lights. ~~dancers.~~

Notice that when shifting the "where" words, the writer decided to substitute more specific verbs for the colorless verb "worked" and to make the picture of "right next to the dancers" more vivid.

The revision shown below is a simple shift of the "why" words:

Original sentence:

The parade was postponed because of the rain.

Marked for revision:

The parade was postponed because of the rain.

The following is an example of a simple shift of the "how" words:

Original sentence:

The building was completed on time by having workers on the job twenty-four hours a day.

Marked for revision:

The building was completed on time by having workers on the job twenty-four hours a day.

In other words, to improve the sentence structure of your first draft

- consider shifts of when, where, why, how words.
- build skimpy sentences and bland sentences with additional details and substitution of colorful verbs for neutral verbs.

GET RID OF TIRED WORDS

Is the word *said* in your composition? Can you substitute a verb that suggests how the words sounded—*whispered*, *yelled*, *hissed*; or a verb that ties in with the message of the words—*warned*, *pleaded*, *boasted*. Is the word *nice* in your composition? Take it out. You apparently wanted to say something pleasant—a nice house, a nice person—so say it. Is the house livable, spacious, comfortable, imposing? Say it. Is the person friendly, kind, generous, fun-loving, considerate, reliable, dependable? Say it. Are the words *big* or *small* in your composition? Take them out and try for words that suggest how big, how small—*enormous*, *gigantic*, *towering*, *huge*, *tiny*, *puny*, *dainty*, *undersized*, *frail*.

You have now done everything you can to meet the standards suggested by the questions on page 70. All that remains to be done is to check for errors in mechanics.

Chapter 8

GOING PUBLIC

Before an edited and revised piece of writing is copied over into its final form, the writer must make sure that no errors in the so-called "mechanics" of writing spoil the well-organized, interesting product he or she has produced.

So you, the writer, look up the spelling of any words you are not sure about. You may ask someone to check your composition for spelling errors. You make sure that you have followed all the rules of punctuation and capitalization that apply to your work.

You have surely heard about, and practiced the use of, the basic rules of punctuation and the basic rules of capitalization. But knowing a rule is one thing; applying the rule as you write is another matter; catching yourself when you have failed to apply a rule correctly is still another matter.

To reassure you that you are familiar with basic rules of punctuation and capitalization, there follow excerpts from earlier chapters of this book, together with some questions about punctuation and capitalization in those excerpts. Try to answer each question by stating the rule that applies in the situation. Then check your answer against the rules that follow the exercise. The rules are numbered to go with the questions.

1 Why this capital letter?

3 Why this comma?

5 Why this period?

6 Why this comma?

Why this comma? (Same rule as #2)

9 Why this exclamation point?

2 Why this comma?

4 Why these apostrophes?

7 Why this capital letter?

8 Why these quotation marks?

If my rich uncle left me a fortune, I sure would have a ball, but I think I'd have sense enough not to act as if there is no tomorrow. The day I really have part of that fortune I'll start off on a spending spree. Every time I have just enough money for one ice cream soda and that rich, chocolaty syrup slides down my throat, I think what it would be like if this could go on and on. So the first money I spend will be to find out what one soda after another tastes like. Then I'll start on the big-ticket items. There's a computer in Hobson's window that takes dozens of games and can do word processing. That's on my list, along with a stereo set for my room. No more "TURN THAT THING OFF" when I enjoy hours of my kind of big-sound music.

Why this capital letter? (same rule as #1)

10 Why these commas?

There simply are not enough lockers in the halls, in decent condition, for the number of students in this school.

Why this period? (Same rule as #5)

11 Why this apostrophe?

Some people might say X's hair is messy, but I think he likes to look casual.

Why this comma? (Same rule as #3)

12 Why these commas?

Your teacher calls attention to an article in the local newspaper reporting on the recent return of Ms. Hermine Jaspar, a retired local business executive, from a trip to Argentina and Chile.

Why these commas? 13

14 Why these capital letters?

We were very much interested, therefore, to read in the Daily Argus of January 10, 19— that you recently returned from a trip to Argentina and Chile.

Why this capital letter? 15

Why these comma? 16

SOME BASIC RULES
ABOUT PUNCTUATION

2. Place a comma after a clause that comes before the subject of a sentence.
3. Place a comma before the conjunction that joins the two parts of a compound sentence, that is, a sentence that expresses two closely related complete thoughts.
4. Use an apostrophe to show the omission of letters.
5. Place a period at the end of a declarative sentence.
6. Use a comma to separate two or more adjectives.
8. Enclose a speaker's words in quotation marks.
9. Use an exclamation point at the end of a sentence that expresses strong feeling or emotion.

10. Use commas to set off words in a sentence when doing so makes the meaning clearer.
11. Use an apostrophe to show possession.
12. Use commas to set off words placed next to a name, or a noun or pronoun, to give information about the person.
13. Use commas to set off a word or words when a slight pause before or after the word(s) would make the message of the sentence clearer.
16. Place a comma between the day and year in a date.

SOME BASIC RULES
ABOUT CAPITALIZATION

1. Capitalize the first word of a sentence.
7. Capitalize the names of persons and places.
14. Capitalize and underline the names of newspapers and magazines.
15. Capitalize names of months and days of the week.

The list of punctuation and capitalization rules could go on, but the sixteen illustrated above are basic. If you

- have a clear understanding of why those rules make sense,

- apply them as you write,

- check yourself to see that you have applied them, your writing will be amazingly free from mechanical errors.

The checkup on mechanics is the next to last step in the writing process. The very last task, of course, is to recopy the work so it can go to its audience.

You, the writer, holding in your hand a piece of writing that you planned, drafted, edited, revised, checked for mechanics, then recopied, have one final question to ask yourself: "Is this the best work I can do?" After an honest "Yes," you can release it to your public with pride.

INDEX

ABOUT THE AUTHOR

Bertha Davis is a former teacher of social studies and department chairman in the New York City school system, and has been a member of the faculty at New York University for sixteen years.

She has written a number of textbooks in the language arts, and is the author of *How to Take a Test* and the coauthor of *How to Improve Your Reading Comprehension*, both published by Franklin Watts.